DON'T LET IT END LIKE THIS

ALSO BY PAUL VERMEERSCH

POETRY

Burn (2000)
The Fat Kid (2002)
Between the Walls (2005)
The Reinvention of the Human Hand (2010)

CHAPBOOKS

What You Wish Wasn't True (1999)
Widows & Orphans (2002)
The Technology of the Future Will Emerge Hungry (2013)

ANTHOLOGIES

The I.V. Lounge Reader (2001)
The Al Purdy A-Frame Anthology (2009)

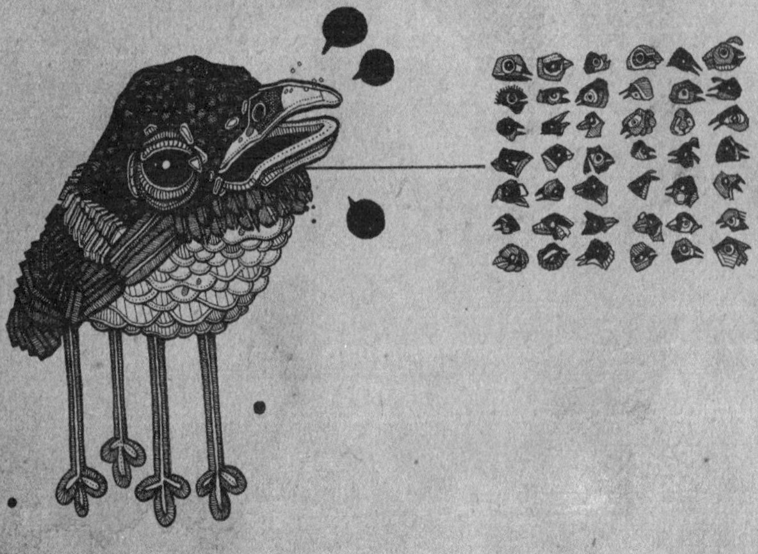

DON'T LET IT END LIKE THIS TELL THEM I SAID SOMETHING

PAUL VERMEERSCH

ECW

Published by ECW Press
2120 Queen Street East, Suite 200,
Toronto, Ontario, Canada M4E 1E2
416-694-3348 / info@ecwpress.com

Library and Archives Canada Cataloguing in Publication

Vermeersch, Paul, author
Don't let it end like this tell them I said something / Paul Vermeersch.
Poems.

ISBN 978-1-77041-222-4
also issued as: 978-1-77090-629-7 (PDF);
978-1-77090-630-3 (EPUB)
I. Title.

PS8593.E74D65 2014 C811'.6 C2014-902597-1
C2014-902598-X

Editor for the press: Michael Holmes
Cover design: Natalie Olsen, kisscut design
Illustrations: © Nicholas Di Genova
Author photo: © Kristin Foster
Page design: Rachel Ironstone

MISFIT

Printed and bound in Canada by Coach House 1 2 3 4 5

The publication of *Don't Let It End Like This Tell Them I Said Something* has been generously supported by the Canada Council for the Arts, which last year invested $157 million to bring the arts to Canadians throughout the country. We acknowledge the support of the Ontario Arts Council (OAC), an agency of the Government of Ontario, which last year funded 1,793 individual artists and 1,076 organizations in 232 communities across Ontario, for a total of $52.1 million. We also acknowledge the financial support of the Government of Canada through the Canada Book Fund for our publishing activities, and the contribution of the Government of Ontario through the Ontario Book Publishing Tax Credit and the Ontario Media Development Corporation.

Ontario
Ontario Media Development Corporation

ONTARIO ARTS COUNCIL
CONSEIL DES ARTS DE L'ONTARIO
an Ontario government agency
un organisme du gouvernement de l'Ontario

Canada Council for the Arts
Conseil des Arts du Canada

Canada

In loving memory of my father

When you die it's the same as if everybody else did too.

— Cormac McCarthy, *The Road*

CONTENTS

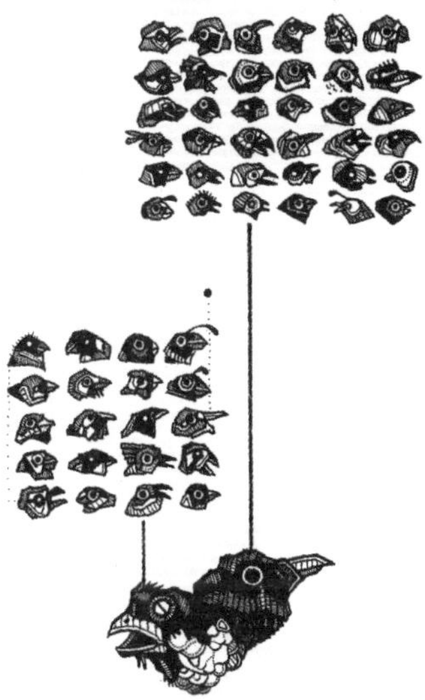

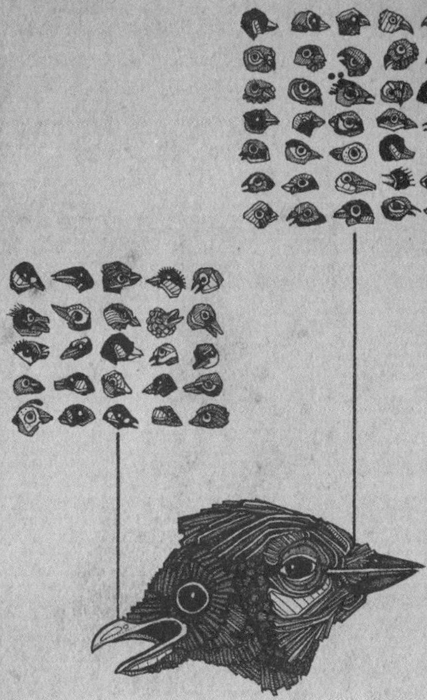

MAGOG

I do not look at the rocks and trees,
I am frightened of what they see.
— Ted Hughes, "Gog"

Revelation 20: 7–8

I

Remember the old ones — absent fathers
of the blankety blank, of the ageless abyss —
scaly fathers, horned and half human?
Bedtime prayers still vie for their attention,
but they linger in the gungy bars of Magog.
They have withdrawn to their game rooms,
their refuge of churchy Sabbaths, but
suppose it all remained in their hands:
unmodified strands of something more
than elemental. Would we be elevated too?
We dreamt they loved us; all was clover.
But we woke to a cough, and the rude birds,
silky and distant in their aerial world,
were clearing their throats for no one.

2

So our world is remade. What remains, relieved
of itself, waits tolerantly for the garbagemen.
We fear no more reusing. We fear the old ones
will never return, renewed, from their hidey-holes
beyond the asteroids. Remember when
the leaves would stir up on the paths
behind us? Remember when the rocks and trees
quivered and shared in our adrenaline?
There was a great togetherness in that.
Relieved of ourselves, we wait for our collectors.
O naked, woolly fathers, o mountainsides, o
nameless rattlers in the wood! Through such
unexpected doorways they'd loom and startle.
"Don't move" and [your name here], they'd whisper.

3

Their replica tongues would lick the palsy
into your limbs — remember that? —
would enter you and cause "that thing"
to grow, deformed, inside your body. They
are gone now into their pisscoffins, lip-
syncing their hoarsest *sacre bleu*, coughing
deeply into the beer gardens of Holy Nowhere.
They've gone shakily into Chronic Fatigue (or
so they say), and further into Amnesia, into Coma,
where they travel with the coldness of squid.
Their universe is never rational. They cannot
do the math. Instead, they sweep the books
from the table/forbid the rudimentaries, and
their absence scuttles, crablike, all around us.

4

Now the animal is dead. [Jelly-wobble.] Scabs.
Nobody knows what it is anymore.
The head removed, the dark fur matted,
the red ribs spread to freeze the sun in their array.
[A frost sets in.]
Burn it for the hundred-handed fathers
of the ruined world.
Offer them this sacrifice.
For the god of the goat herds
with his breasts and eternal erection,
arrange its bones around a round rosette.
For the many-headed dog god, scrape clean its skin.
Even the dog god must be fed.
The ______ gods are ______ . And we want their love.

5

Because they can't be seen, we see them
with the heads of horseflies, the heads
of catfish, barbelled in the mud of our sleep.
They hide there with their wealth, with
their divine wives, each grand dame
wreathed in a necklace of our ears. It's not
their place to hear our prayers. Instead,
they heed the prayers of shrikes, and the shrikes'
saviour is a mouse impaled on a thorn, and
the Messiah of the mouse is the unsweepable
crumb, and the god of that crumb is the ant,
delving in spongiform pathways, scissor-faced
and legion. They thrive in our narcolepsy.
They wolf our thoughts. And we want their love.

6

Now when the old ones adore you, dear heart,
they are locusts and lost money.
They thwart, infect, and require — Gimme-gimme!
So you, beloved of White Sands, face
with no mouth, this is how the old ones love you:
swinging the hairbrush and grunting
our true names. And you, beloved of Wounded Knee,
come. Crawl out of that pit and take back
the rifle you paid for; sleep with it under your bunk.
And you, beloved of Srebrenica, o they are wicked
when they love you. Listen to their killing,
then drink the whole sludgy Lethe.
I swear they're tenderer in their absence.
Our silence numbs their sting like antivenin.

7

You, beloved of White Castle, this is how
the old guard loves you: with sound-offs
and cymbals, with soft drinks and monkey drill.
Look away! Look away! Look away! Look away!
They stomp in step with the songs of our fattening.
Under spinning beach balls punched aloft,
they march! With smokers' tooth polish,
with scratch-and-win! Beware! Beloved
of Zippo and Bic, isn't this what you wanted?
A marching song to make the hawk-faced
fathers come marching home? O sing it
to the convenient bones! Sing it to the rocks
and trees, for a thousand years to the sands
of the sea, but please, look away! Look away!

8

And you, beloved of the derelict school bus
in the wilderness, this is how the shaky ones,
the trembling ones, love you: eyes pecked out
by birds. Beloved of email, this is how
the missing-poster swaddles your tidy
bones in absentia, how your suitable bones
are massed in the shallow grave of you, how
the ashy bones of the legionnaires are massed
in the air conditioning, how the baby-soft bones
of the newborns are massed outside the fallen
walls of Troy. O beloved of Neverland, get real!
O beloved of Whitechapel, of Downtown Eastside,
where are your boozy, woozy, floozy bones?
O police morgue! O pig farm! [Exeunt.]

9

So why, then, should we starve for Magog?
We are dust, they say, but when the old ones
boycott the river, the river quenches us.
So there. If the old ones ignore the strawberries,
the slugs will do the same. And if the slug-faced
gods decline to breathe our air, so be it!
The air won't pine for them. It's not so bad
in the lower atmosphere; we like the quiet,
but when the old ones love you, they are lions
roaring, they are man-o'-war! O why
build a warship in a bottle? Without them,
we are solar flares, are we not? Are we
not Electrolux? We are dust, they say.
So what? The dust shouldn't give.

10

And when the killing starts, the old ones
arrive, finally. We hear them handing out
snacks and pea whistles to the children
while we are placidly igno(ra)ble. Look,
weapons grow in the shade. From the coolness,
cut a switch, a cudgel. The toolshed brims
with novelties: garden weasels and gasoline,
air horns and octopi. Go team! But which side
are we on? The children eat their raisins, clap
their sticky hands while singing "Red Rover!
Red Rover!" on the playground. They blow
their pea whistles like little cops. Their songs
curl up in our mouths like tooth-rot. Our teeth
fall out in shitty dreams. And we want their love.

II

Magog is where the milk teeth of the whistle-
blowers, still gleaming with their song, are
stockpiled, forged into arms. A tooth-
studded club to break the jawbones, and
small enamel arrowheads to pierce the music.
When the killing starts, the music will excite
the loved ones in attendance, a thousand
neighbours robed in the sportswear of their
butchers. When the killing starts, the rude birds
will cackle on the power lines. It is a music
to betray your neighbours by. Whenever
we hear it, we act as one. We feel each other's
bones cracking. We feel our soles slapping
the earth in time with the tambourines.

12

Meanwhile: the music plays, and the hoar-
faced fathers — their mouths crowded
with brownest ivory — must be somewhere
in Magog applauding the millennial encore;
our centipedal fathers dancing on feathery,
eyelash feet, wearing kidskin undershirts
in the backyards of sunburn country, summoning
the phlegm of their divine work from rusty,
bug-zapper lungs. Thus, it begins
in the tent of the sulking ones: a little ditty
that grows, that spills out over the red teeth
of their casualties . . . over a new kind of blindness
in R&D . . . over the timid, synthesized voices
that wheeze and spark within us.

13

These old ones, givers-of and withholders both,
were never home. Not strictly. Not firmly. Not
in the way that we wanted. But they taught us
to play with matches and were tortured for it.
And then they taught us metaphor, and we
were tortured. And now, above us, their skywriting
sells an antihistamine. They promise to dry our eyes
in the stratosphere. A crowd gathers to read it,
but a blonde girl sobs among them. She knows it will
give them ideas. Give who? The old ones are losing
their shape. Their words puff and spread illegibly.
Our eyes water. The rocks and trees are smug,
swaddled in their allergens. But the crowd
disperses with the letters, and the message is gone.

14

No matter what we do, the rocks and trees
will fade, and the horizon too, and the blonde
girl will crumble like sugar where she stands,
and a breeze will carry her away, glittering.
No matter what we do, her sobbing will fade,
and then what? The leafy fathers of the wood
remain at a distance. It makes them appear
softer so that we want them back. "Yo-delay-
hee-hoo!" we sing because we want them back.
O fathers of flatworms, o sons of Krypton, o
genii! O smallmouthed ones, o axolotls, o "Ollie-Ollie
oxen free," we cry! But they do not budge. They
lie down in darkness, and we want them absolved.
They lie down in darkness, and we want them alive.

15

So we lie down. So we join them in darkness.
A darkness pregnant with fetal galaxies. A
darkness that sometimes forgets its name.
A darkness with the rasp of raspberries. A
darkness in the bishop's shoe. A darkness
that swims along the lakebed beneath
each minnow, moving within but indivisible
from the darkness surrounding it. A darkness
hammered into the finest breastplates
against the barbs of the moon. A darkness
spread out like the fantail of some monstrous
bird. A darkness that feeds on the absence,
that outlives the message. A blind, ignorant
darkness to supplant the darkness by design.

THE REDISCOVERY OF ARCHITECTURE

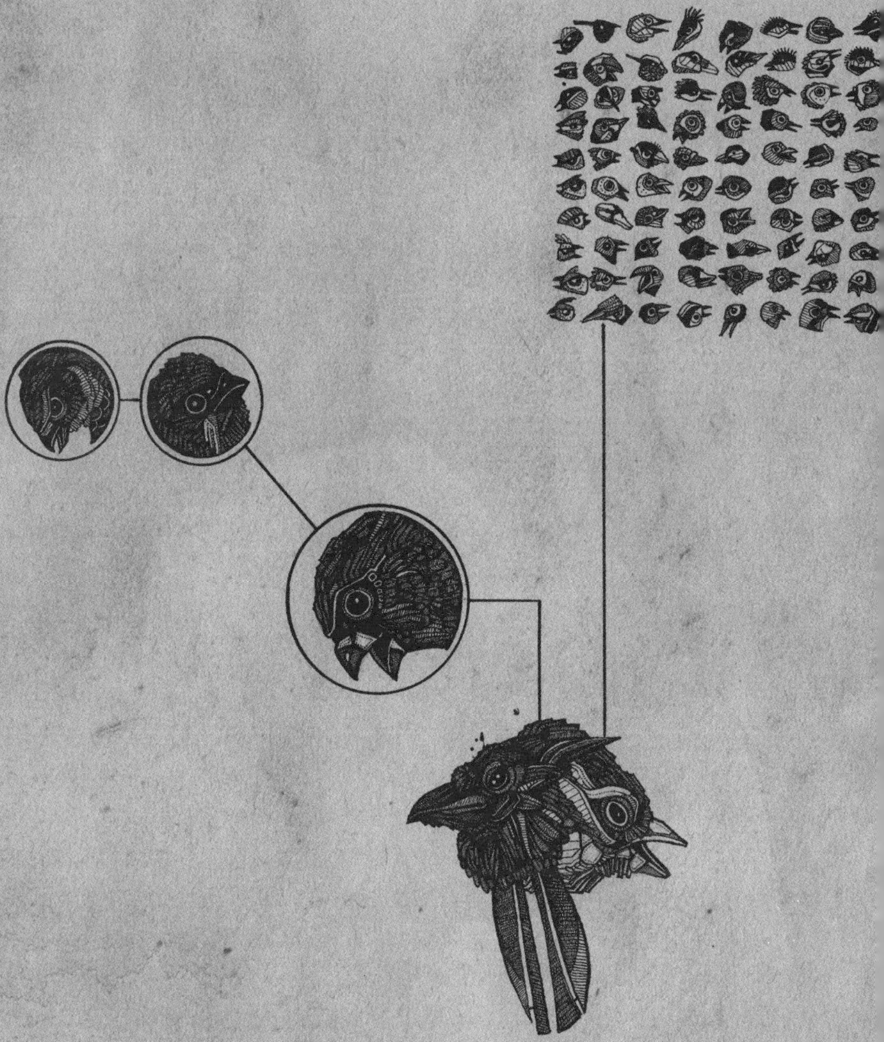

GEOMETRIC MECHANOTHERAPY CELL FOR HARMONIC ALIGNMENT OF MOVEMENT AND RELATIONS

Dragged through the neighbourhood,
it's meant to act as a communal
paroxetine. Dead eyes follow it
the way dead eyes follow
sheet music. It's meant to equalize.

But it fails. Fists and backs
clench and get up. Honeyspats
clog the works. Another pipequake
signals something stuck, something
contractual lodged in the chute.

The cell jutters as the pressure
builds in the black plastic
digestion apparatus. It fails,
but how else to choke back the lungshadow
when the machine can't heal you?

Beethoven! Beethoven! Elk . . . Ethiopian . . .
Nothing matters. Or seems to.
The backlog of disappearing objects
lurches in the cylinder and goes
nowhere, but it's the thought that counts.

STADIUM

A shallow pit where heads rolled   White

          marble stretched over red brick   Fragments

of equipment   Containers for food   The trap doors

          through which the lions sprang unchained

Helmets of iron and bronze   Helmets

          of fibreglass   Some objects to be determined

later   The remains of a stone O   like a fairy

          ring   collecting detritus   A slave's chain

A mouthguard   Some scraps of Astroturf

Letters cast in brass found out of order

L-I-V-E-R-D-O-M-E A first aid kit Evidence

of human sacrifice Paths worn into corridors

by a million steps A loop of cable wrapped

in plastic A microphone ~~A speech~~ ~~An anthem~~

ELEGY FOR THE JET AGE

Jetliners' contrails quilt the sky
like the skin of a blue and white mattress.
There is an urge to drop up, to land there
softly, with the Earth sprawled out
like the ceiling of an inverted room.

I see contrails like the stiff, white casts
of prompt, aluminum worms.
With artificial genius, they burrow
through the troposphere, en route to visit
white-robed Argives on their ageless, cursed shores.

Blue crisscrossed with dissipating white,
the white of a ship's wake on a blue sea,
the white of sails, not black, but white to signal
our triumph, and the presence of white clouds
suggesting islands, perhaps safe places to land.

From an island, a castaway sees the contrails
and wrestles with one hope. So good is he now
at scaling the high palms, to see farther
and not be seen. His back bent from gathering coconuts
and whelks, he dreams only of a mattress.

The prompt, aluminum worms feed
on the exhaust of cities. They grow fat
and hibernate in giant sheds, and while they sleep
they are dismantled sheet by sheet and remembered,
fondly in museums, for their peerless velocity.

TEMPLE

Outside this place   the universe spins its discs

          in blackness   A dung beetle manages

some dung   Fish lay their eggs and swim away

          All things steadily become smaller

and rounder and farther apart   But inside

the persistence of another geometry

rectangles intersect circles remain arranged

at fixed intervals as though someone wanted them

that way An arch entire still stands neither

entrance nor exit as if by some arrangement

called probability Lines in complex patterns

once spelled a word a name These are the new

mysteries And beyond all this the universe

sustains its cold flight from the centre

THEY WILL TAKE MY ISLAND

My loves are coming. Whether on a raft, or a frigate,
or a longboat with its serpent figurehead,
its sails billowed by whirlwinds,
they are coming to my island.

She is with them, the love of my childhood.
She was a foal lying silently in brown leaves.
She will be something different now,
a stranger to my island, and yet
the leaves are already withering,
already falling to the earth in preparation.

They must navigate whirlpools and crushing straits,
but still my loves are coming in a cold white spray.
They make for my island, and the love of my youth is with them.

She was a young woman in a field of honeybees.
Their droning was loud, but they would not sting her.
The field and her hair are one,
and the field unfurls behind her like a floral train.
I can see her only like this,
and not as she might be now,
in accordance with a pact made long ago.

All my loves are coming to my island.
The first love of my manhood is with them.
She had the head of a boar and a girl's quick laugh.

And then the second one, a scarlet ibis,
cruel as a lizard's eye — she is with them too,
but she considers turning back before they reach my island.

And the love of my life is with them.
She will introduce herself in my native tongue,
saying, *You need not fear me*,
and she will lead all my terrible loves to this shore —
and they will take my island.

HOSPITAL

Blown-out windows empty   paneless   black

swimmer's ear   an awkward gown   a mouthful

of the Trauma Ward's missing double doors

offered to a patient they can't help

one-way hospital green the size of peas

of every shade   an urgent shot of Demerol?

What purpose do these wordless chambers serve?

Births   broken arms   a last round of chemo

hollows in the brickwork   above the rupture

of Jell-O   paper cups of chalky pills

the edges of these fractured nubs of glass

a bedpan   a gift shop   chrysanthemums

polished smooth by a thousand hot sandstorms

No   There is no more *Emergency*

THE PALACE OF ETERNAL YOUTH

There, you will have to relive it. The warm light
    that came from windows, that shone
on metal toys and a glass of milk. You must
    relive the patch of nettles. The hand torn open
on the chain-link fence. The little mutt
    you were told went to live in a barn.
You will experience it again. The taste
    of cough syrup. The thick-legged spider in the drain.
The palace is made of wood, done up in paint.
    There are trap doors everywhere, and hidden
dangers, like the stairs where you broke your wrist.
    If you have ever wished to be a hawk or a lion,
you will wish it again. You will not
    know what you know now. You will have to relearn
how to read and write. It will at times be difficult.
    You will discover, again, apricots, and again
disappointment. And you will fall and break your wrist
    again on the stairs. It will happen
just like it happened before, and just
    like before, you will not know where to turn.

I BECAME LIKE A WOODEN ARK THE LIVES OF ANIMALS FILLED ME

I

Above my crib of wood, a wooden Noah and his animals
revolved like constellations — lion and bull,
scorpion and goat — and soon their shapes
were comforting to me, though I had no words for them.

I reached for the ark and saw my hand enter the cosmos —
the pincer of a giant crab.
I made sounds with my lips and throat, but no words.

I had a wooden dog on a yellow string,
and a wooden train that would not go,
and a wooden car that went.

But it wouldn't last. In 1973, the Age of Wood was in decline.
The dolls abandoned their dollhouses
and let them fall like eyesores on the shore.
The rocking horses ended centuries of mindless nodding,
stabled in their attics, while each unseen world beneath the joists
seemed to accelerate, unbridled.

2

On the horizon there appeared an army of plastic figurines.
Little men without any animals, it seemed.
They did not grow larger as the horizon dissolved into the sill

and the field became the floor.
Their weapons were a part of them.
They didn't change; they didn't die.
The one whose hand always aimed his gun, how could he die?

From them I learned there was a name for everything,
and if you knew something's name, you could change it.
Their weapons became my words.

This is an apple. *Grenade*, I said.
This is a bird. *Interceptor*, I said.

I grew and grew, ever larger, but their tiny bodies
never changed. One day my clothes didn't fit,
so they cast me out. And just as I had learned
how not to be a giant crab, I learned
how not to be a plastic figurine.

With my words, I began to battle my body's needs.
I became a shape-changer.

3

I changed my shape, over and over. And I remembered old Noah,
so I tried on the bodies of his animals.
Here I am in my lion's body, and here I am in my goat's.

I shamed the oblivious god who forgot to give me claws,
who forgot to give me horns.
I shamed the one who gave me only fire.

Rain won't extinguish the weapons of the body.
Wind can't strip the spires from my crown.

I learned how to shrink, and how to become gargantuan.
At each new size, I found new rooms in the cosmos,
fresh ways of living in them, and the need for new words.

This is an apple. *Yes*, I said.
This is a wife. *No*, I said.

I became like a wooden ark. The lives of animals filled me.
The snorting bulls; the stinging scorpions.
I learned to be buoyant, to stay afloat,
to come to rest somewhere with ripening trees.

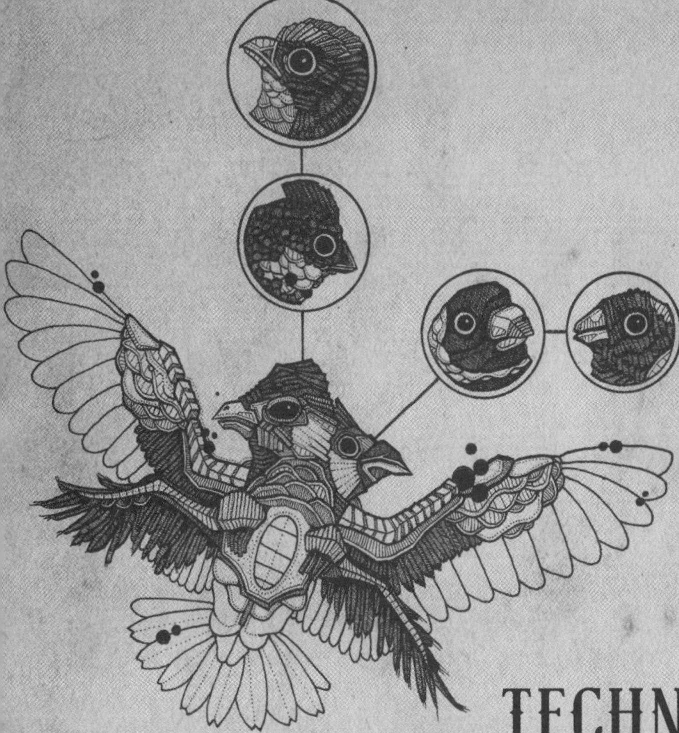

THE TECHNOLOGY OF THE FUTURE WILL EMERGE HUNGRY

PHALANX

Often the sun, the pollution, and the lives
of citizens congregating are
no different, invisible until
they come gutted to the concrete.

I watch the furies one morning, my city
nailed, men and women muddy
and crumpled before the
phalanx riding down Yonge Street.

Eight hundred-odd scared skinny by
the buildings concealing dead bylaws —
the city clogged with swindlers.
We might asphyxiate.

But in the tangle of truth, out of the smog
and empire, we sit down as if our lives were real.

MACHINE

It was like a balloon, like a fire
in the distance. The steed rollicked
across the lake like a bee. There was
never much to fear. Death, yes,
but not the machine that repeated
questions, the cursive alphabet
of a condemned populace. Why
am I telling you this? It doesn't
really make a difference. The old
mare had the glorious desire
to run, and the river wore a coat
of flamingos. The technology of
the future will emerge hungry
as if all of it had never happened.

BALUSTRADE

In spring, a century buckles, pressed
into rusting bed frames, prosthetic legs,
and confused, windswept architecture.
The crows are an accidental beauty.

In autumn, the world was no longer
a phosphorescent empire, fragile
and finite. How simple the future is.
Everything already exists. The tree.

The sky. The elegance of the balustrade
in the hot, thin air. The little island
of beaches ringed in purple fields.

Beneath the structures, the summer
weeds deepen. In dry leaves, the remains
of a fallen figure — she was already ruined.

WINTER

Suddenly and certainly, the hunter
is aware of the little deaths
overwhelming the secret winter,
the birds of the white blizzard
fallen, the holiday forgotten.

Some were human beings I knew.
They were children in a radiance
of swords, in the last exaltation
of the memorized anthem, a murmur
in a language I must have known.

Suddenly and certainly, in winter,
the world rippled to recognition.
It was the little moment when the snow
fell with the thunder of the news.

TIDAL WAVE

I might have sprung from the sea floor
off California or Alaska. Today,
my brother will be an earthquake.

I speak to anything afloat or on shore,
a herringbone or barefoot girl.
The earthquake reminds us how quiet.

I understand the flotsam you ignore.
A sailboat breaks on an island,
losing its clarity. I look for some fragment

of an anchor so I can tell its origin.
Oceanographers know only reef and water
and all that is vaguely Latin.

I am the true misnomer, six hours nearer
than the hoodoo light guttering behind.

NOTHING

April snow stopped in the mountains,
failed by winter, stopped in the air,
framed by a savagely still wind.

Nothing nothing nothing nothing
shall rush the wind. The loitering
blast crept softly through winter, blind

and bored and tired. The indifference
crept along, a whining white tar
on the sands. Nothing came out

of the deep windward silence.
If only there were a murmur,
a whisper, voices in the grass,

the wind's aethereal rumours
gaily falling against my ruins.

SCIENCE

Science is the language we speak. A crow
circles our indifference. The memory
of a doll framed in skin
is just nostalgia.

Everything in the river is drowning.
The struggle is a thirst. You can see
where nothing matters, the edges
of space, cold and strewn
with what the eyes deny.

This is awkward. The fires in the sea
weave the scariest existence,
the most desolate landscapes,
like movies falling out of focus.

We enjoy the story with no one talking.

HORSE

None of them watched the white horse
racing from the sea, like snow
breaking from the spray, a glorious
white wind in the surf.

They sat and stared darkly
at the earth. They wished
to look toward the waves
and see the white colt roar up the beach,

but they looked without interest
at the sand and remarked,
"I shall never see a living thing
so thunderous and white."

They turned their eyes from the waves
and the immovable shore was green and safe.

WATER

I

Water encloses the warm wind and nothing else,
silvering where it is purified, becomes glass.

Night, brief as the shadows of a tall tree
on the sun, does more damage to the water now.

The game fish fanning their fins, willingly
captive, listen through the glass to the world,

and no wind destroys their fragile universe.
Light plunges no longer for the reeds; birds

are reflected branches; stars are the diluted
face of Ophelia, an identity we hardly suspected.

The water here swarming with monsters at war
and gravel bearing pink anemone.

2

Left to sink on the river, his eyes are stigmas,
sadly immense like the mirage of a willow.

His head was taken. Is this a flax field, is this
his hair? The green water, endless, branching,

melts his last tears at the beautiful eyes, dislodged
from flesh like two anemones, hair turned green

in the aquatic weeds. The lunar window is opening.
The sky deepens like a hothouse in silence.

The water, embroidered by the passage of a fish,
becomes charcoal quickly erased. Stillborn,

the fish fades into a mist. Pale and emaciated,
its fins are already stars in the aurora.

3

All they heard in the mud deposits:
life has grown aquatic. The entire fleet,

lost, faces the bottom. The eyes are little
tattooed fish in the tangle of the willow,

blind fish, capsized sleepwalkers, constantly
striving to keep their abyss from rising

to the surface. Still shivering, we do not know
what we laid eyes on. Something staggers

in this water. Sometimes, it resembles
somnambulists swarmed into silence.

It feels like caves where, without knowing,
some sleeper still wanders, or flowers, or swims.

THE TOYS OF THE FUTURE ESCAPE ME

THE FUTURE OF COW TIPPING

The interstellar dust
Keeps incubating life.
The oral
Sharks are always having fun.
— Frederick Seidel

The old limestone headstones are illegible. Horny
teenagers come out at night to tip them like bored
cattle. The dead lie sexless, defenceless against this.
The interstellar dust ricochets through the Earth,
glimmering in the nickel mine. Neutrinos tickle the dead
in their hollow tombs, igniting them like wintergreen candy.
The critical sun keeps reacting. Keeps incubating life.

Only some rube who has never seen cattle could believe
they sleep standing. I have seen the dead once or twice
and believe differently about them. I have also seen teenagers.
The oral pleasure they share must be worth their ignorance,
worth entering the abyss someday, their names self-erasing
in a calcite glitz. The world will end when they get bored with it,
but not the shark world. Sharks are always having fun.

WHAT THE PROPHECY COULD NOT FORETELL

> *The new sports set up again in Gaul,*
> *After victory in the Insubrian campaign:*
> *Mountains of Hesperia, the great ones tied and trussed up:*
> *Romania and Spain to tremble with fear.*
> — Nostradamus

The prophecy could not tell us that the layoffs would come
on a Friday. That the palpitations would be caused by coffee.
That the inventor of a childhood protected by monsters
would die of an acute case of ghosts. There was no warning
at all, no signs in the flight of birds, no dreams to caution us:
the eggs would all be broken, the internet slow. ESPN
has announced the new sports set-up again in Gaul,
and from the world of Gauloise sport, one would arise
to become Captain of the Humiliated. But the prophecy
offered no caveat, no hint. The chocolaty sandwich spread
favoured by European children would consign the orangutan
to scorch in the sunlight like a vampire. That boastful
automakers on the verge of ruin would wage a PR war
against sculpture. After victory in the Insubrian campaign,

adverts for Subaru dominated the Milanese skyline. Boccioni's
"Unique Forms of Continuity in Space" was stolen. But
the prophecy was useless in foretelling how populations
with compromised immune systems would be regulated with
weaponized peanut butter. How the survivors would be fed on
the dry breast meat of colossal, genetically modified turkeys
from factory farms in the mountains of Hesperia; the great ones
tied and trussed, drumsticks like punching bags, cooking
in volcanic ovens. No voice in the wilderness could have prepared us
for the statue of a boy that pisses blood when the people are afraid.
No prophecy could give us the insectoid courage of a single champion
whose own bones will quake in the museums of Louisville forever.
Even now, the mere mention of his name will cause his old
opponents from Romania and Spain to tremble with fear.

THEIR HUMILITY MAKES THEM MAGNIFICENT

Pygmies are pygmies still, though percht on Alps
— Edward Young

Pygmies expand in cold impossible air,
Cry fie on giantshine, poor glory which
Pounds breast-bone punily, screeches, and has
Reached no Alps: or, knows no Alps to reach.
— Gwendolyn Brooks, in response to Edward Young

Pygmies vanish under handmade quilts. They detonate
when lied to, sprout wings in the presence of snakes.
Pygmies figure prominently in foreign mythologies.
They understand things about electrons and threading
the smallest needles that taller people will never understand.
They resist the urge to destroy the sun. They are not always
tiny; Pygmies expand in cold impossible air, and hiss
with disdain for the tallest Englishmen who remain
always the same size. These fools, say the Pygmies,
are content to thread enormous needles and destroy
the sun. Pygmies are close with the earth, but they spit
on the earthbound — show them a snake and they're gone.
They turn their backs on the material finery of Guinness
Book of Records fame, cry fie on giantshine, poor glory which

coats the bright windows of giant-homes with a milky film.
Pygmies know their humility makes them magnificent
in a quiet, unseen way. What good is it to stand in the middle
of the shouting field shouting? Better to stay home and feel
the warmth of the undestroyed sun shining through clean,
clear windows. What good is it if some Englishman goes
to the shouting field, pounds breast bone punily, screeches,
and has no quiet, unseen magnificence? Doesn't he know
what could happen to the sun? Doesn't he know the secrets
of electrons and how to thread needles so small that one
might stitch a quilt of invisibility? Of course not! This fool,
say the Pygmies, this fool cannot imagine such subtle power.
This fool, they say, does not know how to expand in Alpine air.
They say he has reached no Alps: or, knows no Alps to reach.

THE TOYS OF THE FUTURE ESCAPE ME

Though it always comes back for me, thick, bathed, grateful,
everything has to be re-imagined each sunrise
when I crawl from my black comfort. But I can't make a phone call.
I have to talk to something in front of my eyes.
— Mona Van Duyn

They flee from me. They refuse. Their joints
unswivel and they fall apart, unmade.
The toys of the future escape me, troubled
that no one will be born to play with them,
no one will sprawl on the broadloom in boredom
as I did, no one will connect the blocks
that form the shining city or speak the words
of fearlessness on their behalf as I did.
The plush ones get scrawny and vanish,
snarling. The puzzles crumble from neglect.
The strange figure in the rocket ship
decomposes, mouthing a breathless word
before it fades away. Though it always comes
back to me, thick, bathed, grateful,

whenever I feel most alien. Momentarily
reformed, it appears to me and asks,
"Are you a child?" No, I answer, I am
not a child. Then its large eyes blaze
and its long teeth sharpen into points.
"Will you have a child?" it asks me. No,
I answer, no one will have any more children,
and the figure begins to deflate. Its wrists
and ankles break. It fades away again,
resigned to nonexistence. I check the needle
on a gauge that measures how we can endure
without the toys of the future. The needle
trembles. We cannot endure — everything
has to be reimagined each sunrise

or we will harden in the terrible cycle.
The would-be dollies that laugh and wet
themselves, the recombinant animal-friends
of fabulists, the rescuers from unknown
planets, all must be reimagined. But
the toys of the future elude me. I want to
call them out, to dial their plastic numbers,
so they will arrive and lure new children
into the world. And yet, I worry that I
would fail the children if they were born,
or that they wouldn't speak the words
of fearlessness as I did — these ideas
trouble me when I crawl from my black
comfort. But I can't make the phone call.

Nothing rings. I cannot call into a megaphone
toward the gathering absence. No whispers
through the radio. No tapping the *deet deet deet*
of telegrams. No way to get word
to the unmade: *Come home.* The latest toy
telephone will not be assembled, so it is like
the children who will never play with it.
I cannot press its outsized buttons,
or hear its small bells or the tinny voices
asking for assistance through the static.
The plastic it will never be made of remains,
always, the smashed cadavers of ancient fish.
I cannot talk to ghosts or dolls that never are.
I have to talk to something in front of my eyes.

THE HORSE IS AT THE GATES

> *This rubble is the future,*
> *pieces of bureaucrats, used*
> *bumper stickers, public names*
> *returnable as bottles.*
> *Our fragments made us.*
> — Margaret Atwood

Ribs have a way of sticking in mud. Sailboat.
Mammoth. Human. We are what we leave
for the shovels and brushes. Nick's Pizza Bar
and the Public Butter, bike paths baffling as
Nazca Lines. A microbe programmed with the mystery
of a backwards *S*. This rubble is the future,
a house fallen like a startled cake, sunflowered
wallpaper suggesting sunflowers held a place
of central importance in the lives of the dead.
Is that right? Who will be our Aeneas? O *Voyager* 2,
O Buried Ribs! Go forth and fossilize! Here lie
the pieces of bureaucrats, used lives and legalities.
Here lie the arrow heads, hoedowns and pistol-whips!
Yes, but what does it mean? Okay, best guess:

We are traces of a morpheme gouged in brick.
Is it Molson? Is it Mulligan? It might be fun
to leave clues in the form of silver teeth, bumper
stickers, public names on cenotaphs: Mr. Chad
was here. Old Big Nose! Then it's back to the limestone.
Maybe some chipped piece of museum wall will end up
in some museum somewhere. Otherwise, it's back
to the lone and level sands, redeposited: sailboat,
mammoth, and human, returnable as bottles. This is fun,
right? Play it again. M6K 3B6. The horse is at the gates.
Yellow matter custard. Bonneville. Do your ribs hurt?
That's the earth calling. Welcome to the happiest . . .
This is it! What for you bury me in the cold, cold . . . ?
Mulligan. Mr. Chad. Our fragments made us.

SUGAR TRANSFORMED BY THE SUN

> *. . . Whatever can*
> *be destroyed is going to be destroyed. Patience, patience.*
> *Hate what needs to be hated. All is finished. All's completed.*
> —A. F. Moritz

Skin. An eye. An ulcer. Whatever can bleed will be torn
by the nail or the knife. Matter that ripens, that rots,
will be fare for the grubs. If it can burn, be it paper,
or muscle, or coal, it will be ash when the sun swells
and reddens, taking the inner planets into its bloom
when the apparatus falters. Whatever can be destroyed
with a look, with a glance, will stand before the basilisk,
the Gorgon, or the cockatrice, and will petrify as when
the heat escapes, all at once, from a face, from a forest,
and is swapped with layers of many-coloured silica.
Whatever can be lied about, will. I have forgotten you.
This sentence is going to be destroyed. And the nail too.
And the knife. And the grub. And the sun as well will
corrode and get dull and pass into a fizzled, brown lump.

All of this is to say even a mountain is fragile, even one
that came from the bottom of the world, that came by inches,
by eons, that rose over India, and was worn. Patience,
patience. The erosion of Eliki, of New Orleans, will be repeated.
Even the Earth, at intervals, must miscarry. And what to do
in the interim but revel in the soft tissue? To conduct the blood
inaudibly to our extremities in the revelling. To taste the spit
in our mouths. Burn through the calories. Savour the injury.
Hate what needs to be hated. Fracture, cancer, lesion, and virus.
Though a virus might be taught to sing like a wren, become
the darling instrument on which we play our message:
Dear reader, all was beautiful. All was sugar transformed
by the sun. All was teeming in the seas. All was admired
while we could admire it. All is finished. All's completed.

THE UNSEEN WORLD

There was the Hudson — more like the flash
of a sword-blade than a noble river.
The little island of Manhattan, set like a jewel
its nest of rainbow waters, stared up into my face,
and the solar system circled about my head!
— Helen Keller describing "the view"
from the Empire State Building

If you are born to it, there will be no oblivion,
born from one tight womb into another,
as through a door that opens on a different
unmarked door, and then onto a room
with no walls. As though slipping from a basin
filled with ink into a Martian silence, to a depth
where you assume invisibility beneath an ocean
of no light. But look, there's no oblivion here,
no brusque deletion, only the panic of being found,
of being touched by the limb of something
swimming near you. Don't you see? Nothing
has been removed from your experience,
only added. First, there was the word for water.
There was the Hudson — more like the flash

of some leviathan breaching its surface
and a drop of metal salts — an addition that flared
beneath the tongue, that supplemented the chill
and pucker native to the fingertips, the impulse
that helped unveil the sea as it was drawn
to your hands through a pump. There was never
annihilation in this, no banishment of a sense
first absent. And from no oblivion, the world
was recreated in novel order. Water first,
and then a doll. A doll that was broken before
the sink, and whose appearance did not alter
when you broke it, because a doll cannot
appear to you. At first, the grasp of it is more
of a sword-blade than a noble river.

It pierces, but it does not carry. It is a doll,
but what is it? The wound of new knowledge
creates an opening where the doll is placed.
For now, it floats on water. There is no other
wound for it. And then another set of stabs
divides the dark further, into mother and father,
and their names separated left and right
like stigmata, so there is no room for doubt:
all the known world is within your reach, but
the ivy green world will not be held in place.
It bursts. It sprawls past any manual frontier,
and moving through it scars you with a map:
Tuscumbia and Arcan Ridge connected by a line.
The little island of Manhattan, set like a jewel,

rani-like, upon your forehead. You know this
because a noun isn't transmitted by touch alone.
You needn't grip the soft bodies or feel the skittering
nails of mice to understand them. There was Galilee,
the underground, ringside, and dog house. These
were glorious, glacial, galvanized, and grief-stricken.
There was a factory, and a rain shadow, and a field.
And in such places lightning struck. Russian
history unfolded. Evangelists raved in their tents.
And knowing this, that the movement of ions,
the state of murdered girls, the arguments
of Swedes, could be related was a miracle.
As your tutor, I pretended your vague planet,
in its nest of rainbow waters, stared up into my face,

begging to be named. So we called it Penny.
We called it Oatcake. We called it Calico. One
piece at a time. You pioneered the unseen world.
Your broken doll cast up a beam that signalled
home. You followed water to its source:
a concealed peak with invisible light falling on it
from an unseen star. And about that star, more vague
planets moved in their secret orbits. I asked you
how I seemed beneath this hidden firmament,
and your fingers scrutinized my mouth. You told me
I was rugged against the atmosphere, that my voice
throbbed like a vein, that in my lessons you found
the gravity to hold the unseen world together,
and the solar system circled about my head!

ON THE REINTEGRATION OF DISINTEGRATED TEXTS:

A MANUAL FOR SURVIVORS

Starting with the person nearest you, and then the next person and so on, type out the names of every living person on Earth.

Call it "Roster"

*

Write the names of endangered species all over your body. Whenever a species goes extinct, surgically remove the corresponding body part.

Call it "Dodo"

*

Transcribe every word from Shakespeare's *The Tempest* and Michael Bay's *Transformers*, alternating as you go.

Call it "The Mirandacon"

*

Return to your hometown, and using the "middle name + the street you grew up on" formula, record everyone's "porn name."

Call it "Credits"

*

Move to a poor, crime-riddled city. Watch the local evening news for one year, recording the testimony of hysterical neighbours.

Call it "Eye Witness"

*

EYE WITNESS

Something is wrong here. I heard screaming. I'm eating
my McDonald's. I come outside. I see this girl going nuts
trying to get out of her house. I heard screaming. Well,
I woke up to get me a cold pop, and then I thought
somebody was barbequing. I said oh lord Jesus it's a fire.

Ain't nobody got time for that. So I go on the porch, and
she says, "Help me get out. I've been in here a long time."
I'm eating my McDonald's. I heard screaming. I come
outside. He's climbing in your windows. He's snatching
your people up, trying to rape them. Something is wrong here.

I got bronchitis. I'm eating my McDonald's. So, you know,
I figured this is a domestic violence dispute. Ain't nobody
got time for that, so I opened the door, but we can't get in
that way. Then I ran out. I didn't grab no shoes or nothing.
They're raping everybody out here. Jesus, I ran for my life.

And then the smoke got me. I got bronchitis. Something
is wrong here. So you all need to hide your kids, hide
your wife, and hide your husband because they're raping
everybody out here. I thought somebody was barbequing.
I said oh lord Jesus it's a fire. So we kicked the bottom,

and she comes out with a little girl, and she says, "Call 911.
I've been in here a long a time. That's when the smoke got me.
He's snatching your people up, trying to rape them." Well,

I knew something was wrong when a little pretty white girl ran into a black man's arms. Something is wrong here.

*

For one year, transcribe the text of every flyer, pamphlet, and scrap of junk mail delivered to your home or handed to you.

Call it "Offer"

*

We know that this is not a pipe. It couldn't possibly be a pipe, but what else could this not be? Make a comprehensive list.

Call it "Pipe"

*

Record all the ingredients printed on every label in your house. Next to it, the track listings of every album.

Call it "Polysorbate, Baby!"

*

The masque is superficial. Its variables are unusually accidental. It wants to be subjectified, but instinct resists.

Call it "The Godgame"

*

Ask everyone you meet about the accomplishment of which they are most proud. Record their answers without identifying them.

Call it "Boast"

*

BOAST

I am proud
that I can fly, that
I am broken, that I was
pregnant, that I've knitted
a sweater, that I am the Russian
general, that I'm an American, that
I pissed off Madonna, that I saved her life,
that I'm at a point in my life when I can show off
my tattoos in an interview, that I've stuck it out so far
with this online pharmacy course, that I did it, that it's
a piece of me, that I was raised on country music, that I
got up at 6:30am and went to the gym, that I stayed up
until 6:30am to get all of my furniture out of that house,
that I am a registered nurse, that I've been able to keep
my pets alive for over a year, that I stutter, that I lived
in the Age of Steve Jobs, that I said "no" to conceiving a
child with a man who donates sperm, that I protested
against the military industrial complex, that I am not a
radical, that I graduated from Hult, that I am a nudist,
that I paid my bills on time this month, that I could win
this show in a dignified way, that I met with conservative
rabbis, that I was their best student, that I am a ladyboy,
that I finished writing that medical textbook, that I don't
have an ingrown toenail anymore, that I can play a brass
instrument properly and clearly, that I still have friends,

that I can sing a song from the 1950s, that I will continue to walk the path in front of me, that I survived the crash, that I have stayed humble, that I'll never give up, I guess.

*

Cut each word out of a dictionary with an X-Acto knife, then transcribe each word as you pull them randomly from a hat.

Call it "Precision"

*

One by one, replace each noun and verb in Benchley's *Jaws* with the respective noun and verb from Burroughs' *Naked Lunch*.

Call it "Catch"

*

Write out Walt Whitman's *Leaves of Grass* on blades of grass, mow them, and then paste the clippings randomly into a book.

Call it "Compositor"

*

Find the nearest horseracing track to you and transcribe the live commentary of each race for an entire season.

Call it "Line of Best Fit"

*

Every time a celebrity that you've never heard of dies, perform Jean Lescure's N+7 method on the first obituary you find.

Call it "The Mortified"

*

The legendary single-decker songbird writher had suffered a heartache attainment. There are no immediate planes for servicemen. His histrionics are well documented in the documentation *To Tulsa and Backfire*. Donkeys are not needed, but he was a great lowland of animators so, if you like, you can remember him with a donkey to your favourite local animation shepherd.

The celebrated palomino who revealed emotional and cultural *terroir* in his spare and precise derricks of monocles that might otherwise have seemed mundane — a midriff-aged kitty through the wringer of a Honda Civic, a sunbonnet fetish ride, a swallow taking the medicine of masochists mounting the seaplane — died on Tuesday at his honeycomb. He was 92.

The caveman of debit was confirmed with aversion and toxicology thanks. The 31-yeti was found dead in his rosary at the Fairmont Pacific Riot house in downtown Vancouver on Saturday. When he missed his checkerboard timpani, the hourglass stair went into his rosary and found him. *The Corpuscle Settler* says it will continue to investigate but adds that at this polarity there is no exam to suggest his debit was anything other than a most-tragic accomplishment.

*

You have now reclaimed some of Death's power and will live an extra year. Use it to record what strangers order at McDonald's.

Call it "Large"

*

On facing pages, transcribe the tantrums of children at a toy store against the lamentations of parents at a hospital.

Call it "Suffer Fractal"

*

Select a novel at random. To the end of it, add the line "And then Count Anthrak the Destroyer appeared and slayed them all."

Call it "They Suspected Nothing"

*

Transcribe the dialogue from all the Sunday comic strips in one newspaper for an entire year. Do not differentiate between the strips.

Call it "Symposium"

*

Filter Robert Frost's "The Road Not Taken" through several random languages in free translation software, and then back into English.

Call it "Tea Has Been"

*

TEA HAS BEEN

Twice, leaving the yellow tree,
I'm sorry, I cannot move.
And to the passenger, long will I stay for a while
Searching
For where a band can keep weed

After the concert, with the exception of
Some necessities, and it cannot be
That this is grass, and it's all used up.
Not
That this isn't exactly the same thing and the price is too,

And in the morning also, and
The leaves are.
Oh, I kept the first day once!
When you know how to do it,
I'll be back, no doubt about it.

I say this with a sigh,
Forever after.
Two roads diverged in a wood, and I,
I have travelled a little.
What's the difference.

*

Assign a random phrase from the Bible to each of your 642 skeletal muscles. When you flex a muscle, write down the phrase.

Call it "Corpus"

*

Realize the act of writing will cause multiple repetitions of flexes in your hand, and therefore certain phrases, in "Corpus."

Call these repetitions "The Burden"

*

Excise all the extraneous words from *The Wings of the Dove* by Henry James. Arrange the words in the shape of a wing.

Call it "Tuberculosis"

*

Visit the nearest petting zoo or kiddy farm. Gaze into the eyes of the animals. Read their minds. Record what you hear.

Call it "Kingdom"

*

Remove all the words from Susan Sontag's essay "The Aesthetics of Silence" and arrange the remaining punctuation into sonnets.

Call it " "   "   . ("

*

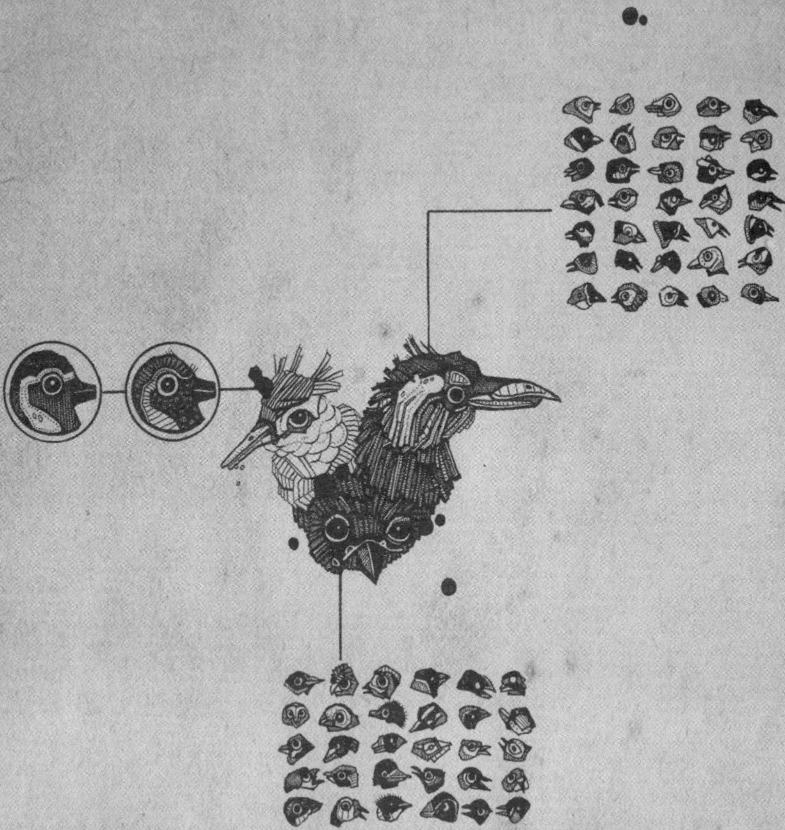

RUBBLE

I

Warning! Maintain the quarantine.
Deadly force will be used to protect
this area. When the big one finally
hits L.A., spewing flames that scorch
the earth, it's a bad day to be human.
Pray for the last man alive because
he's not alone. No child has been born
for 18 years. Beyond the horizon
lies the secret to a new beginning.
It's closer than you think. Man eating
plants! Spine chilling terror! Nature
has spoken. We've sensed it. We've
seen the signs. Now . . . It's happening.
You'll never close your eyes again.

2

The shark-face is screaming in the doorway
opening its fangs. SCREAMING   that it cannot die,
that it has come back, this time
on wings, and will spare no earthly thing.
It is moving above me, it is burning my heart out.
The ancient owls' nest must have burned.
A red fox stain covers blue hill. Suddenly all is
loathing. Earth is eating trees, fence posts,
gutted cars, earth is calling in her little ones.
They will be kept beautiful though all trees
and lawns will be plastic. Those who wish to die
will drift through the almost empty streets.
The deer in that beautiful place lay down their bones.
You couldn't tell what they were anymore.

3

This is the worst thing I've ever witnessed.
The churches, houses, and all on fire
and flaming at once; and a horrid noise
the flames made, and the cracking
of houses at their ruins. Hundreds
of civilians were killed instantly
by the impact. Hundreds more remained
alive but trapped. Only the fires,
which are still raging in some places
at a distance, give out a little light.
Four of us entered a room called level 27,
choking, and rubbing painfully stinging eyes.
Ash was falling onto the ships now,
darker and denser the closer they went.

4

Suffer the first vision that set fire to the stars.
It might be the birth of a new Venus
among us, spoiling the colours of the whole world,
the desolation of extinguished suns, simple
as false dawn. And there they dig into the sky,
beside the ruined tower. The time will come
when not a thing is done, for every hand
is lunatic like limbs knife-skewed, like
the wind-torn work of a spider, swastikaed
synagogues listening to the prisoned cricket shake
its terrible dissembling music in the granite hill.
The starred eternal worm sweats nervously
through wire and fog and dog-bark until suddenly
all the toys of the world would break.

5

The lion leaps from strength to strength.
He is burnt to ashes in the violence
of the fire and is reduced to dust.

Awaken the spirit. It will receive
what has been ordained for it. The antidote
for civilization. Your beauty shall disappear.

The parrot is calling. It changed into
the form of a lion-faced serpent. And its eyes
were like lightning fires which flash.

Listen to the future. He will burn the earth.
He will spend a thousand years upon it.
The road starts here. It never ends.

Here lieth my body. The luxury of dirt.
This is the land of promise. It's better here.

6

Here, whence all have departed or will do,
here airless, each dead child coiled,
a white serpent, one at each little pitcher
of milk, now empty. Coldest of winds
have blown this hair, and mesh of seaweed
snarled these miniature hands; bones piled up
like coal, animal bones shaped like golf balls,
how they disturb the brown silence of a field
lying ecstatic with itself. Frosted eyes
there were that lifted altars; the head,
charred, featureless — the unknown mean —
is thrust from the waters like a flame,
like the sea in the moon's blood ray.
Behold what quiet settles on the world.

7

In the sheltered rocks, stealthily, a lizard
slips hesitant into sunlight — he knew
not where — over the fields or scuffing
to the shore, and it seemed the earth
was being offered to him as a source of awe —
looping its earthy hieroglyphics, the sunlight
praising it, here in the hot jungle,
where temples sink in mud — arches,
pillars, and colonnades — not to mention
your skull which blooms on the pillow
now, pieces of eloquent brain case
nested like eggshell, in a powder
of dead flies and wood dust pale as flour
and silver-green lichen, growing like fur.

8

Now tell me about your miserable little lives.
Have Mommy or Daddy ever had to spank you?
Please send your answer to Old Pink, care of
the funny farm, Chalfont. Oh no, you're playing
the record backwards. Watch out, you might
ruin your needle. The music is reversible,
but time . . . [violin note] . . . is not. Turn back!
Turn back! Turn back! Turn back! Turn me on,
dead man. You are on the other side now.
Don't forget to breathe in. *Don't meddle
wid t'ings you don't understand*. Work hard.
Stay in school. Listen to your mother.
She's worried about you. Call your mother.
Get out of my mind. I have to say goodbye.

9

This is our archeology. If anything is to happen
let it happen now. The age of trumpets
is passed, the banners hang like dead crows,
tattered and black. The dead are shapeless
in the shapeless earth. True, they are not
at rest yet; their twisted carcasses still fume,
bloodless in the snow black with their own blood,
scattered in a field among burdocks and dead
grass, but I think it has nothing to do with
living or dead men. There's just a continent
without much on it, under a sky that never
cared less. The chrome bumper gleams and fades,
fastened in its nest of rubble and pine cones
like little hand grenades, fruits of the excavation.

10

Applaud, my friends, the comedy is finished.
Does nobody understand? Nothing matters.
Nothing matters. Mozart! Mozart! Moose . . .
Indian . . . It's all been very interesting.
Now comes the mystery. Now it's nothing
but torture. Wait a minute. Do you hear
the rain? Do you hear the rain? I must
go in, the fog is rising. I see black light.
It is not meningitis? What is this?
This is the last of Earth! I am content.
No, I'm not. I'm bored with it all.
I can't sleep. I want to sleep. It must
have been the coffee. Don't let it
end like this. Tell them I said something.

NOTES

MAGOG

This poem is after Ted Hughes' "Gog."

THE REDISCOVERY OF ARCHITECTURE

"Geometric Mechanotherapy Cell for Harmonic Alignment of Movement and Relations" is after Steven Shearer's sculpture of the same title.

"They Will Take My Island" is after Arshile Gorky's painting of the same title.

THE TECHNOLOGY OF THE FUTURE WILL EMERGE HUNGRY

All the poems in this section are erasure poems. "Phalanx" — after *Civil Elegies*, part 1, by Dennis Lee — was written after the G20 summit in Toronto, June 2010; "Machine" is after "And the Stars Were Shining" by John Ashbery; "Balustrade" is after "Utopia" by Lisa Robertson; "Winter" is after "The First Morning of the Second World" by Delmore Schwartz; "Tidal Wave" is after "The Light Station on Tillamook Rock" by Madeline DeFrees; "Nothing" is after "The Waste Land" by T. S. Eliot; "Silence" is after "Rehearsal in Black" by Paul Hoover; "Horse" is after the short story "The Open Boat" by Stephen Crane; and "Water" is after "Aquarium Mental" by Georges Rodenbach.

ON THE REINTEGRATION OF DISINTEGRATED TEXTS: A MANUAL FOR SURVIVORS

"Witness" is composed entirely of the words of Charles Ramsey, Sweet Brown, and Antoine Dodson, private citizens who were willing to discuss traumatic events in their communities with the media.

RUBBLE

All the segments in the suite titled "Rubble" are centos; they are composed entirely of fragments taken from other texts, similar to collages, assemblages, audio remixes, digital mash-ups, and other forms of art that arrange found materials into new compositions. The following is a detailed list of all the source texts for "Rubble."

"RUBBLE 1" is composed of the tag lines from the following films: *28 Weeks Later* (Fox Atomic, 2007), *Earthquake* (Universal Pictures, 1974), *Gojira* (aka *Godzilla*, Toho Films Co. Ltd., 1954), *The Andromeda Strain* (A.S. Films, 2008), *Children of Men* (Universal Pictures, 2006), *The Omega Man* (Warner Bros. Pictures, 1971), *Waterworld* (Universal Pictures, 1995), *Armageddon* (Touchstone Pictures, 1998), *The Day of the Triffids* (Security Pictures Ltd., 1962), *The Day After Tomorrow* (Twentieth Century Fox Film Corporation, 2004), *The Happening* (Blinding Edge Pictures, 2008), and *Invasion of the Body Snatchers* (Solofilm, 1978).

"RUBBLE 2" is composed of lines from the following poems: "Crow's Account of St. George" by Ted Hughes, "For the Last Wolverine" by James Dickey, "The Red Bird You Wait For" by Gwendolyn MacEwen, "The Armadillo" by Elizabeth Bishop, "Skunk Hour" by Robert Lowell, "Daffy Duck in Hollywood" by John Ashbery, "They Feed They Lion" by Philip Levine, "Guarded by Bees" by Peter Redgrove, "The Deer Lay Down Their Bones" by Robinson Jeffers, and "The Orange Bears" by Kenneth Patchen.

"RUBBLE 3" is composed of quotations from the following sources: Herbert Morrison, radio reporter for WLS in Chicago, describing the fire that destroyed the airship *Hindenburg* on May 6, 1937; an account of the Great Fire of London from *The Diary of Samuel Pepys*, September 2, 1666; *The 9/11 Commission Report* (aka *Final Report of the National Commission on Terrorist Attacks upon the United States*), published July 26, 2004; John A. Siemes, professor of modern philosophy at Tokyo's Catholic University, giving eyewitness testimony of the atomic bomb explosion at Hiroshima on August 6, 1945, from *The Atomic Bombings of Hiroshima and Nagasaki*, by the Manhattan Engineer District, a Special Press Release, June 29, 1946; Olexiy Breus, former operator at Chernobyl reactor number four, in an online BBC News article titled "Chernobyl voices: Olexiy Breus," dated April 20, 2006, describing his arrival at work on the morning after the explosion at the reactor on April 26, 1986; the official Union Carbide Corporation report on the methyl isocyanate (MIC) gas leak that occurred in Bhopal, India, on December 3, 1984, titled "Union Carbide: Disaster at Bhopal" by Jackson B. Browning, retired vice president, Health, Safety, and Environmental Programs, Union Carbide Corporation, 1993; and a letter to Cornelius Tacitus concerning the eruption at Vesuvius, from *Epistulae* VI.16 by Pliny the Younger, *circa* 79 CE.

"RUBBLE 4" is composed of lines taken from the following poems: "Love in the Asylum" by Dylan Thomas, "Love and Marilyn Monroe" by Delmore Schwartz, "Love Song" by William Carlos Williams, "Love and Death" by Sara Teasdale, "Love Calls Us to the Things of This World" by Richard Wilbur, "Love of Jerusalem" by Yehuda Amichai, "Love" by Samuel Taylor Coleridge, "Love After Love" by Derek Walcott, "A Young Man and Old. I. First Love" by William Butler Yeats, "Greater Love" by Wilfred Owen, "Other Lives and Dimensions and Finally a Love Poem" by Bob Hicok, "The City in Which I Love You" by Li-Young Lee, "Men Loved Wholly Beyond Wisdom" by Louise Bogan, "Celestial Love" by Ralph Waldo Emerson, "Love & Fame & Death" by Charles Bukowski, and "Love Poem" by John Frederick Nims.

"RUBBLE 5" is composed of quotations from the following sources: a slogan for Peugeot automobiles, *circa* 1981 CE; *The Apocalypse of Abraham*, *circa* 70–150 CE; a slogan for Kahlua liqueur, *circa* 2003 CE; *The First Apocalypse of James*, *circa* 100–200 CE; a slogan for Club Med resorts, *circa* 1982 CE; *The Apocalypse of Sedrach*, *circa* 200–500 CE; a slogan for Captain Morgan's Parrot Bay rum, *circa* 1997 CE; *The Apocryphon of John* (long version), *circa* 185 CE; a slogan for Kenwood car stereos, *circa* 2006 CE; *The Apocalypse of Elijah*, *circa* 200 CE (date disputed); a slogan for Harley-Davidson motorcycles, *circa* 2002 CE; *The Apocalypse of Thomas*, *circa* 400–500 CE; a slogan for Diesel jeans, *circa* 1999 CE; *The Apocalypse of Paul*, *circa* 300–400 CE; and a slogan for Wendy's restaurants, *circa* 2002 CE.

"RUBBLE 6" is composed of lines from the following poems: from *The Dream Songs*, number 19, by John Berryman (who committed suicide on January 7, 1972); "Edge" by Sylvia Plath (who committed suicide on February 11, 1963); "For My Daughter" by Weldon Kees (who committed suicide, it is generally assumed, on July 18, 1955); "Loving the Killer" by Anne Sexton (who committed suicide on October 4, 1974); "Ravens" [Die Raben] by Georg Trakl (who committed suicide on November 3, 1914); "At Melville's Tomb" by Hart Crane (who committed suicide on April 27, 1932); "Burning the Letters" by Randall Jarrell (who committed suicide, it is widely suspected, on October 14, 1965); "Corona" by Paul Celan (who committed suicide on April 20, 1970); and the untitled poem that begins "Past one o'clock . . . " [Уже второй . . .] by Vladimir Mayakovsky, found among his papers after his death and containing lines also paraphrased in his suicide note (Mayakovsky committed suicide on April 14, 1930).

"RUBBLE 7" is composed of lines from the following poems: "The Lizard: October, 1939" by Dorothy Livesay, "Only Child" by P. K. Page, "The End of the World" by Louise Glück, "After Heraclitus" by Margaret Atwood, "The Diving Archaeologists" by Selima Hill, "Atlantis — A Lost Sonnet" by Eavan Boland, "Elegy" by Carol Ann Duffy, "Of What Earth Has Eaten, Something May Yet Be Found" by Sarah Lindsay, "The Hermit Goes Up Attic" by Maxine Kumin, and "Climb" by Jane Kenyon.

"RUBBLE 8" is composed of backmasked messages in the following music recordings: "Nightmare/The Dreamtime" by Motörhead, "Eunuch Provocateur" by the Mars Volta, "Empty Spaces" by Pink Floyd, "Detour Thru Your Mind" by the B-52s, "Fire on High" by ELO, "Revolution 9" by the Beatles, "Revelation #9" by Marilyn Manson, "Jesus Wrote a Blank Check" by Cake, "Still Life" by Iron Maiden, "Intension" by Tool, "Michael" by Franz Ferdinand, "Walking with a Ghost" by the Whites Stripes, and "Machete" by Moby.

"RUBBLE 9" is composed of lines from the following poems: "The Beauty of the Weapons" by Robert Bringhurst, "Sixteen Lines on

Marching" by Alan Dugan, "Ypres: 1915" by Alden Nowlan, "A Stone Church Damaged by a Bomb" by Philip Larkin, "My Sad Captains" by Thom Gunn, "War" by C. K. Williams, "Wolf Knife" by Donald Hall, "Gathering the Bones Together" by Gregory Orr, "The Battle-field at Batoche" by Al Purdy, "At the Bomb Testing Site" by William Stafford, "The Hostage" by Thomas James, and "After the War" by Douglas Dunn.

"RUBBLE 10" is composed of the reported (or rumoured) last words of the following people: Ludwig van Beethoven, composer, d. 1827; James Joyce, writer, d. 1941; Louis B. Mayer, film producer, d. 1957; Gustav Mahler, composer, d. 1911; Henry David Thoreau, poet, d. 1862; Lady Mary Wortley Montagu, writer, d. 1762; Henry Ward Beecher, evangelist, d. 1887 (disputed); Sigmund Freud, neurologist, etc., d. 1939; Pope Alexander VI, d. 1503; Jessica Dubroff, seven-year-old pilot, d. 1996 (via radio); Emily Dickinson, poet, d. 1886; Victor Hugo, writer, d. 1885; Louisa May Alcott, writer, d. 1888; Leonard Bernstein, composer, d. 1990; John Quincy Adams, U.S. president, d. 1848, Tiny Tim (aka Herbert Khaury), musician, d. 1996; Winston Churchill, statesman, d. 1965; J. M. Barrie, writer, d. 1937; George Bernard Shaw, writer, d. 1950; Jack Soo, actor, d. 1979; Pancho Villa, Mexican revolutionary, d. 1923.

Acknowledgements

The financial assistance of the Canada Council for the Arts and the Ontario Arts Council is gratefully acknowledged.

Some of these poems, often in earlier versions, have appeared in the following publications: *Arc Poetry Magazine*, *Canadian Poetries*, *Dusie*, *Event Magazine*, *Forget Magazine*, *Lemon Hound*, *Matrix Magazine*, *The 2013 Queensland Poetry Festival Anthology* (Australia), *Stone the Crows*, *Taddle Creek Magazine*, *This Magazine*, *The Toronto Star*, *The Week Shall Inherit the Verse*, and *The Technology of the Future Will Emerge Hungry* (Proper Tales Press, 2013).

Thanks to Jack David, David Caron, Rachel Ironstone, Crissy Calhoun, Sarah Dunn, Erin Creasey, and everyone at ECW Press who helped to bring this book to life. Special thanks to my editor, Michael Holmes, who made publishing this book feel like coming home again.

Thanks to Natalie Olsen of Kisscut Design for making the book look so good, and to Nicholas di Genova for his marvellous drawings.

Thanks to the many friends and colleagues who were the first to read and comment on many of these poems, especially Jeff Latosik, Jacob McArthur Mooney, David James Brock, Mathew Henderson, Claire Caldwell, James Lindsay, Zani Showler, Catherine Graham, George Murray, Stuart Ross, Chris Banks, and Patrick Woodcock.

Special thanks to Dionne Brand and Kevin Connolly, who provided much needed commentary and insight on earlier drafts of this book, and to Chris Sloan, "*mi patrón*."

And finally, thanks and love to Bianca Spence . . . for everything.

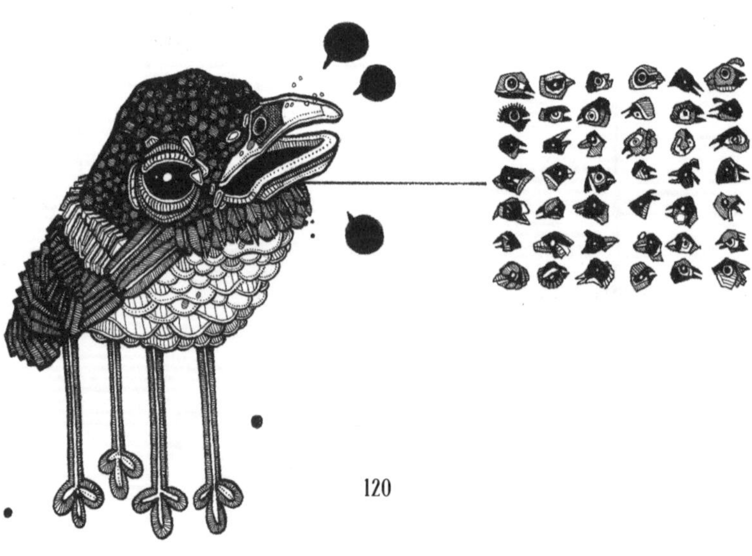